Geography Starts

GLACIERS

Claire Llewellyn

Heinemann Library
Chicago, Illinois

Designed by David Oakley
Illustrations by Hardlines and Jo Brooker.
Printed by South China Printing Co.(1988) Ltd, Hong Kong / China

04 03 02 01 00
10 9 8 7 6 5 4 3 2 1

Library of Congress Cataloging-in-Publication Data
Llewellyn, Claire.
    Glaciers / Claire Llewellyn.
       p. cm. – (Geography starts)
    Includes bibliographical references (p.) and index.
    Summary: Introduces glaciers, describing the different types, their formation, their effect on the land, and their benefits.
       ISBN 1-57572-205-4 (Library binding)
       1. Glaciers—Juvenile literature. [1. Glaciers.] I. Title. II. Series.

GB2403.8.L554 2000
551.31'2—dc21
                            99-053324

Acknowledgments
The Publishers would like to thank the following for permission to reproduce photographs:
Ecoscene/Graham Neden, p. 8; Ecoscene/Andrew Brown, p .10; Ecoscene/Sally Morgan, p. 29; FLPA/Mark Newman, pp. 6, 18; FLPA/W. Wisniewski, p. 11; FLPA/S. McCutcheon, p. 17; FLPA/Keith Rushforth, p. 19; NASA/Johnson Space Center, pp. 22, 24, 26; Oxford Scientific Films/Doug Allan, pp. 9, 13; Oxford Scientific Films/Frances Furlong/Survival Anglia, p. 14; Oxford Scientific Films/Kim Westerskov, p. 15; Oxford Scientific Films/Godfrey Merlen, p. 16; Robert Harding Picture Library/Roy Rainford, p. 5; Robert Harding Picture Library/Kim Hart p. 7; Science Photo Library/David Vaughan, p. 20; Science Photo Library/J. G. Paren p. 21; Still Pictures/B. &C. Alexander, p. 4; Still Pictures/Theresa de Salis, p. 12; Still Pictures/Roland Seitre, p. 28.

Cover photograph reproduced with permission of Still Pictures.

Every effort has been made to contact copyright holders of any material reproduced in this book. Any omissions will be rectified in subsequent printings if notice is given to the Publisher.

Some words are shown in bold, **like this.**
You can find out what they mean by looking in the glossary.

Contents

What Is a Glacier?

A glacier is like a river of ice that flows very slowly over the land. Glaciers are found in the coldest parts of the world.

This glacier is in Greenland.

This glacier is on Mont Blanc, the tallest mountain in France.

Glaciers are also found at the tops of the world's highest mountains, where it is always very cold.

How Are Glaciers Made?

Glaciers start in places where it often snows. The air is so cold that the snow does not melt. It piles higher and higher on the ground.

A lot of snow falls in the French Alps.

This glacier is moving down
the mountain and into a lake.

At the bottom of the pile, the snow is
squeezed into ice. Over thousands of
years, the ice becomes very thick and
heavy. It slowly starts to move.

Sheets of Ice

This **ice sheet** is very thick. It is almost covering the mountains.

There are two kinds of glaciers. Some glaciers are thick sheets of ice, like pancakes. They cover the land in the coldest parts of the world.

An ice sheet always flows toward the sea. Here, it breaks up into huge chunks of ice that crash into the water. They are called **icebergs**.

Most of an iceberg is underwater.
It may take years to melt.

Valley Glaciers

The other kind of glacier is called a **valley glacier**. These start in small valleys in the mountains. They move slowly downhill.

The moving ice can change the mountain's shape.

This icy stream is flowing from the tip of a glacier in Norway.

The end of a glacier is called the **snout**. Here, the ice melts into a cold mountain stream. Glacier water is often full of bits of rock that have been worn away.

The Surface of a Glacier

The surface of a glacier is not smooth. There are many cracks, called **crevasses**, in the ice. The deep cracks show the clean, blue ice below.

The surface of a glacier can be dirty.

These rocks were carried along by the moving ice.

A glacier picks up rocks that lie in its path. The rocks rise to the surface as the glacier moves along. The glacier can move huge rocks a long way.

Changing the Landscape

Long ago, the Earth was colder, and glaciers covered more of the land. They carried rocks, which scraped the land and changed its shape.

A glacier dug out this deep valley in New Zealand.

This fjord is in New Zealand. It was once a valley in the mountains.

The glaciers cut deep, wide valleys in the mountains. Some of these valleys have been flooded by the sea. They are called **fjords.**

Rocks on the Move

These huge rocks were dumped by a glacier.

Glaciers carry huge rocks as they move. When the ice melts, these rocks are left on the land. They may have come from a long way away.

Most of the rocks are left on flatter land. In some places, they have made high ridges and hills.

This small hill is in a valley in Alaska. It is really a pile of rocks dropped by a glacier.

Fresh Water

This river is pouring from a glacier. It makes a good home for many animals.

A lot of fresh water is frozen inside a glacier. When the ice melts, the water flows into lakes and streams. These are homes for animals and plants.

Mountain rivers are always full of water. The **energy** of the flowing water can be used to make **electricity**. Power stations like this one are built in the mountains.

As the water moves along, it drives machines in the power station.

Studying Glaciers

Scientists who study glaciers are called **glaciologists**. They measure how thick a glacier is and how fast it is moving.

This scientist is camping on a glacier while working there.

A glaciologist in Antarctica collects an ice sample.

Studying glaciers is important. Glaciers can tell us what the weather was like in the past. They can tell us more about the story of the earth.

Glacier Map 1

This is a photo of mountains. It was taken from a **satellite**. There are **valley glaciers** in the mountains. The mountains lie near the **coast**.

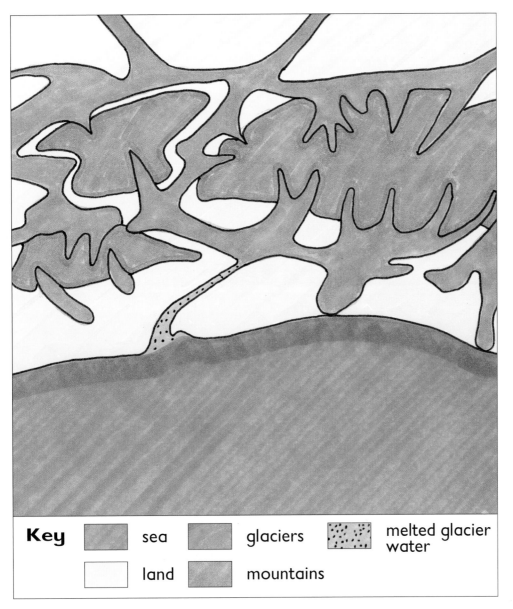

Key sea   glaciers   melted glacier water

land   mountains

Maps are pictures of the land. This map shows us the same place as the photo. We can understand the map by using the key.

Glacier Map 2

This photo shows the same place. It shows a smaller part of the land, but you can see it more clearly. There are lakes on the flatland near the **coast.**

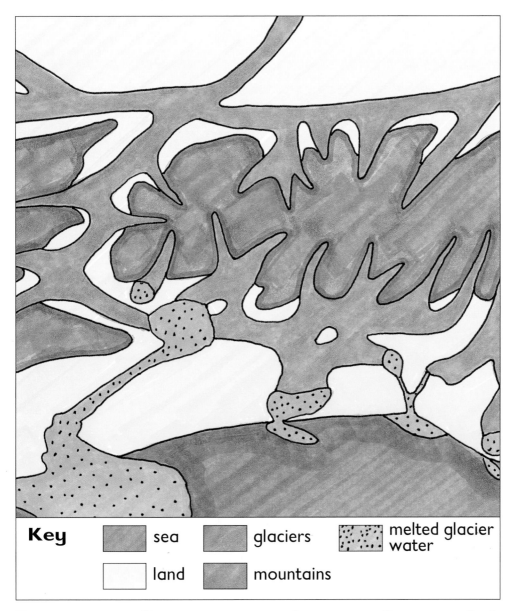

Key
- ▨ sea
- ☐ land
- ▨ glaciers
- ▨ mountains
- ▨ melted glacier water

Rivers are flowing into the sea. Some of the river water is icy blue. It makes light blue areas in the sea. This is water that has melted from glaciers in the mountains.

Glacier Map 3

This photo shows only some of the mountains and lakes, but they look a lot bigger. You can see the glaciers very clearly. There is a lot of snow.

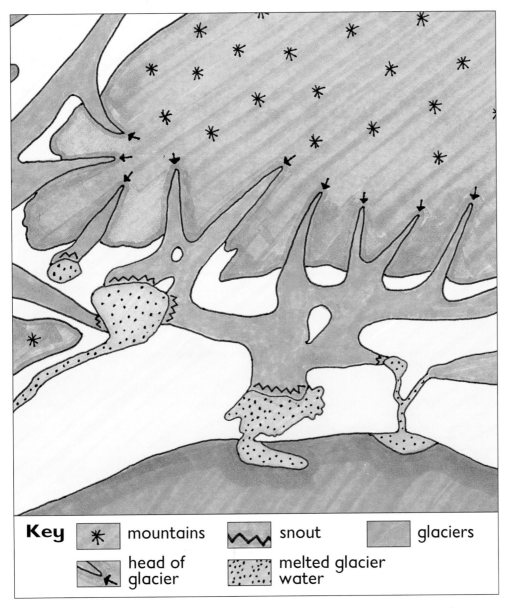

Key
- ✳ mountains
- ᐯᐯᐯ snout
- ▢ glaciers
- ◥ head of glacier
- ⣿ melted glacier water

This map shows the whole glacier and points out some of its different parts. The head of the glacier is marked with an arrow. The wiggly lines mark the snout.

Amazing Glacier Facts

The largest glacier in Iceland is as big as all the glaciers in Europe put together. It is also about three times the size of Rhode Island.

People can visit the Athabasca Glacier in Canada. They take a bus ride over the ice on a part where there are no **crevasses**!

Glossary

coast land that is at the edge of the ocean

crevasse deep crack in the ice (You say kra-VASS.)

electricity power that makes appliances, such as lights, televisions, and radios, work

energy ability or power to do work

fjord mountain valley that was made by a glacier and has been flooded by the sea (You say fee-yord.)

glaciologist person who studies glaciers (You say glay-she-AH-lo-jist.)

iceberg large chunk of ice that has broken off a glacier and fallen into the sea

ice sheet flat glacier that covers the land

satellite special machine that goes around the earth in space taking photographs of the earth

snout bottom end of a glacier

valley glacier steep glacier that starts in a space between two high mountains (You say VAL-ee GLAY-shur.)

More Books to Read

Fowler, Allan. *Icebergs, Ice Caps & Glaciers.* Danbury, Conn.: Children's Press, 1998.

Markert, Jenny. *Glaciers & Icebergs.* Chanhassen, Minn.: The Child's World, 1994. An older reader can help you with this book.

Owen, Andy, and Miranda Ashwell. *Mountains.* Des Plaines, Ill.: Heinemann Library, 1998.

Patchett, Lynne. *Glaciers.* Mahwah, N. J.: Troll Communications L.L.C., 1997. An older reader can help you with this book.

Index